The Biggest Invasions

Of

Mexico's drug cartels

Ryan Chavez

TABLE OF CONTENT

INTRODUCTION

The Drug Cartel Threat in Mexico

The drug cartels have been Mexico's most powerful foe for decades, tearing apart its social structure, undermining its government, and leaving a bloody wake in their wake. These criminal groups, often known as "cartels," have become some of the most powerful and well-known organisations in Mexico as a result of their use of strategies that range from coercive control to open invasion of territory.

With the help of "The Biggest Invasions of Mexico's Drug Cartels," we travel deep within the war that helped to create the current Mexico. This book digs deeply into the background, tactics, and effects of the most infamous drug cartels that have invaded the country and permanently altered its society, economy, and system of government.

We shall see the emergence and demise of cartels like the Zetas, Sinaloa, Knights Templar, and Jalisco New Generation as we examine the pages that follow. We'll delve into the bloody wars, bold power struggles, and territorial disputes that have shaped their pasts. We shall see the events that rocked Mexico to its core, from the bloody streets of Ciudad Juárez to the lavish mansions of Culiacán.

However, there is more to this tale than just strife and violence. We'll also look at how resilient the Mexican people are, what law enforcement is doing, and how the drug trade is supported internationally. We'll examine the socioeconomic effects of cartel activity and the problems that result when criminal gangs have a major influence in a community.

The complicated web of control, corruption, and survival that defines the world of Mexican drug cartels will be revealed in these pages. We'll talk about the continuous conflict between cartels and the government, as well as the initiatives to lessen their power.

The documentary "The Biggest Invasions of Mexico's Drug Cartels" ultimately serves as a reminder of this issue's intricacy and the demand for a thorough knowledge. It is an appeal to acknowledge the seriousness of the situation, take lessons from the past, and make plans for Mexico's future that will make it safer and more affluent.

Join me as we explore a disturbing yet fascinating period of Mexican history that continues to influence the country's present and future.

CHAPTER 1

The Zetas Cartel's Daring Power Plays

Few names in the extensive history of Mexico's drug cartels evoke the same level of dread and interest as the Zetas. This chapter explores the origins of the Zetas cartel, as well as its development and the bold power manoeuvres that contributed to its reputation in Mexico's criminal underworld.

Sources and Formation

A group of elite military personnel turned out to be the source of the Zetas cartel, which was quite surprising. This specialised team was made up of former members of the Mexican military's special forces and was initially created as the Gulf Cartel's enforcement arm. Their tactical skill, discipline, and training laid the groundwork for one of Mexico's most fearsome criminal organisations.

"Ascend to Prominence"

The Zetas cartel swiftly established its supremacy as it grew stronger through a succession of strategic and ruthless moves. Unprecedented levels of violence characterised their strategy, which terrified both opponents and communities. They used strategies like beheadings, mass executions, and power manoeuvres that demonstrated their utter contempt for authority.

Confrontations with Authority

The Zetas were unique in that they were prepared to take on both rival cartels and the Mexican government directly. In their pursuit of dominance, they frequently engaged in violent territorial conflicts that spread across entire territories. Their blatant assaults on military, law enforcement, and government employees had the goal of undermining the state's authority and control.

invasion of other countries

The Zetas cartel elevated the idea of a "invasion" to new heights. By aggressively encroaching on the territory of competing cartels, they virtually annexed entire regions and increased their power. They were able to cement their control over important drug trafficking routes thanks to this tactic.

Effects on Mexico

Bold power moves by the Zetas sparked a wave of bloodshed that rippled throughout Mexico. Communities were constantly in a state of terror as the cartel's presence hampered normal life. The nation was permanently damaged by their use of pressure and intimidation, which had significant social, economic, and political repercussions.

CHAPTER 2

Strategies for Dominance and Expansion of the Sinaloa Cartel

Few organisations have exercised the level of domination and influence that the Sinaloa Cartel has in the history of Mexico's drug cartels, which has undergone constant change. This chapter explores the development of the Sinaloa Cartel, its plans for growth, and the strategies that helped it become a major player in the world of organised crime.

Initial Activities and Origins

The Sinaloa state's vast plains, which have a long history of drug cultivation, are where the Sinaloa Cartel first emerged. Under the direction of Joaqun "El Chapo" Guzmán, what started as a loose network of traffickers transformed into a close-knit organisation. The cartel's early activities were centred on smuggling drugs across the border between the United States and Mexico, especially into the United States.

El Chapo's Premonition

The Sinaloa Cartel implemented a strategy that prioritised horizontal integration under El Chapo's direction. The Sinaloa Cartel tried to cooperate with numerous criminal organisations rather than exterminate them, in contrast to certain other cartels. Through this strategy, they were able to build a sizable network of associates, which in turn increased the cartel's strength and influence.

Geographical Expansion

The Sinaloa Cartel had a diversified approach to growth. It involved expanding its influence throughout all of Mexico and abroad in addition to retaining control over its own region. The cartel's relationships and the assistance of corrupt officials helped it penetrate new areas. This gave them the opportunity to take over important drug trafficking routes and develop a presence in untapped areas.

Violence Under Control

The Sinaloa Cartel preferred to maintain some amount of control over its use of violence, in contrast to some of its more violent rivals. El Chapo was aware of the need to limit carnage to prevent unwarranted attention from law enforcement. The cartel was able to preserve some stability in the areas it controlled thanks to this strategic approach.

Corruption and Infiltration

The Sinaloa Cartel's capacity to penetrate law enforcement organisations, governmental institutions, and other prominent sectors was a crucial aspect of its power. The cartel made sure that little interfered with its activities by taking advantage of corruption. The cartel's control over its holdings was further strengthened by this invasion.

Economic Implications

The economic impact of the Sinaloa Cartel went beyond drug trafficking. It participated in money laundering and other illicit operations while controlling a sizable chunk of Mexico's drug trade. This enormous riches provided the cartel with the means to increase its operations, keep up its power, and win the devotion of a network of allies.

CHAPTER 3

Knights Templar Cartel's Challenge to Authority

The Knights Templar Cartel is a singular and enigmatic force in the complex world of Mexico's drug gangs. This chapter explores the Knights Templar's ascent, rebellion against the ruling class, and unique style of criminal activity that set them apart from their contemporaries.

Ideology and Emergence

Out of the ashes of the La Familia Michoacana cartel, the Knights Templar Cartel rose, first presenting itself as a "self-defense" organisation. By calling themselves after the Knights Templar, a Christian order from the Middle Ages, they acquired an air of chivalry and righteousness. This symbolic decision was supported by a twisted worldview that fused criminal intent with religious zeal.

Territorial exploitation and control

The Knights Templar broadened their scope of operations to incorporate a wider range of illegal activities, in contrast to other cartels that concentrated primarily on drug trafficking. In addition to controlling drug supply routes, they also controlled extortion, illegal mining, and other illegal activities. They were able to harvest resources from the areas they controlled because to their varied strategy.

Confronting Authority

The Mexican government as well as competing cartels were boldly contested by the Knights Templar. They used harsh tactics to demonstrate their dominance, including as public killings and the leaving of grisly warnings for rivals. They aimed to become more than just a criminal organisation by becoming the de facto rulers of the areas they governed.

Impact on Communities

The efforts of the Knights Templar to win the respect and loyalty of local populations stood out as a distinctive feature of their operations. They marketed themselves as guardians, offering services like security and infrastructure upgrades that the government frequently failed to provide. They were able to carry on their criminal activities while maintaining a facade of legitimacy thanks to this tactic.

Corruption and Infiltration

The Knights Templar were excellent at infiltrating governmental organisations and law enforcement organisations, just like other cartels. They were able to elude capture and continue their operations because of the crucial knowledge that this corruption gave them. They were also able to exploit the system to their benefit, which strengthened their hold on power.

Internal Conflict and Decline

The lofty plans of the Knights Templar Cartel ultimately resulted in internal strife and discord. As competing factions arose, the level of violence increased inside the organisation. The cartel's demise was influenced by this internal conflict as well as government initiatives to weaken their influence. Resolute opposition to the Knights Templar's challenge to authority resulted in their steady deterioration.

CHAPTER 4

The Jalisco New Generation Cartel's Quick Ascension to Power

The Jalisco New Generation Cartel (CJNG) has emerged as a formidable power in the dynamic world of Mexico's drug gangs. This chapter explores the CJNG's quick rise to power, its methods for seizing control, and the broad effects it has had on Mexico's criminal underworld.

Leadership and Foundation

The Milenio Cartel, which disintegrated in the late 2000s, served as the genesis of the CJNG. The CJNG was established by Nemesio Oseguera Cervantes, popularly known as "El Mencho," with the intention of becoming a major force in Mexico's drug trade. El Mencho's ferocity and leadership would be crucial to the cartel's rapid expansion.

Wars over territory and expansion

The CJNG has followed an aggressive expansion plan since its founding. The cartel swiftly seized control of important drug trafficking routes and began to compete with other organisations for dominance. Their willingness to engage in vicious territorial conflicts showed how determined they were to seize a sizable portion of Mexico's illegal drug trade.

Highly Complex Operations

The CJNG stands out for its expertise in logistics, technology, and global connections. The cartel used cutting-edge communication technologies and cutting-edge weapons to organise its activities. It was able to sustain a competitive advantage thanks to its flexibility in adjusting to new forms of communication and transportation.

Problems with Authorities and Rivals

Confrontations with both other cartels and the Mexican government characterised the CJNG's emergence. High-ranking authorities, law enforcement agents, and competitors were targeted by the cartel, which used violence to establish its control. The CJNG frequently engaged in violent altercations with authorities, leaving a path of damage in their wake.

Global Reach

The CJNG displayed a willingness to spread outside of Mexico's boundaries, unlike many other previous cartels. The cartel's influence spread to Europe, the United States, and other regions of Latin America. Their global links made it possible for drug delivery networks to traverse continents.

Economic Influence and Power

The CJNG's quick ascent gave them tremendous economic clout. They expanded their criminal activities, taking part in kidnapping, extortion, and other illegal crimes. They were able to influence government officials and broaden their influence thanks to their financial clout.

CHAPTER 5

The infamous Battle of Culiacán

Few incidents in the history of Mexico's drug cartels have garnered as much international interest as the Battle of Culiacán. The dramatic and unusual confrontation between law enforcement and the Sinaloa Cartel in the city of Culiacán is revisited in this chapter to discuss its significance and the reverberations it has on Mexico's criminal underworld.

Context & Background

The Mexican government's efforts to apprehend Ovidio Guzmán López, one of Joaqun "El Chapo" Guzmán's sons, led directly to the Battle of Culiacán, which took place in October of [year]. The operation was a component of a larger effort to topple the Sinaloa Cartel, which had long ruled Mexico's criminal underworld.

Extreme Confrontation

Ovidio Guzmán was under attack from government authorities, and the Sinaloa Cartel retaliated with extraordinary ferocity. A wave of violence was sparked by a series of planned attacks and roadblocks carried out by cartel members around Culiacán. Both the people and the government were taken by surprise by the confrontation's sheer size and ferocity.

Authorities in Crisis

The Culiacan incident highlighted a serious conundrum for the Mexican government. Authorities decided to release Ovidio Guzmán in an unprecedented move to stop more carnage after witnessing the cartel's fierce response. This action raised questions about the government's capacity to uphold order and uphold the law in the face of cartel resistance.

Strong Show by the Cartel

The Battle of Culiacán was a public spectacle that demonstrated the Sinaloa Cartel's bold might in addition to being a conflict between law enforcement and a criminal organisation. The cartel's capacity to mobilise resources, stir up trouble, and obtain the release of one of its leaders demonstrated how powerful it was in the area.

Impacts and Consequences

The conflict's aftermath sparked concerns about the government's tactics and ability to successfully take on organised crime. Some people viewed Ovidio Guzmán's release as a sign of weakness, while others thought it was a shrewd move to stop any future casualties. The catastrophe compelled the nation to assess the state's capacity to handle the cartels' obstinacy.

The Battle of Culiacán marks a turning moment in the history of Mexico's drug cartels, sparking introspection and calls for reform. Law enforcement, public image, and governmental policy were all affected, showing the complex power relationships between cartels and the state.

CHAPTER 6

Cartel Jalisco New Generation vs. Sinaloa Cartel Rivalry

The rivalry between the Cartel Jalisco New Generation (CJNG) and the Sinaloa Cartel has come to characterise a new age of conflict in the always changing chessboard that is Mexico's drug cartel landscape. This chapter examines the strategic manoeuvres, geographical conflicts, and ramifications for Mexico's criminal underworld in the two major cartels' escalating rivalry.

Emergence of the Conflict

It was inevitable that the CJNG would come into contact with the Sinaloa Cartel as it gained strength as it climbed to prominence. Both cartels competed ferociously for control of lucrative drug trafficking routes, which paved the way for a conflict marked by territorial disputes. The criminal environment in Mexico would be forever changed as a result of this titanic struggle.

Power plays and strategies

The CJNG and Sinaloa Cartel's conflict intensified as a result of their ongoing power struggles. Each cartel competed to outwit the other, competing for control of important routes used for drug trafficking and growing their respective zones of influence. These strategies frequently resulted in bloody confrontations and an increase in cruelty as they battled for dominance.

The conflict over Jalisco

Jalisco, the home state of the CJNG, became the centre of contention as both cartels fought for control of this vital region. Unprecedented violence was unleashed during the ensuing fights, inflicting havoc on nearby communities and testing the government's ability to keep the peace. Power was relentlessly sought after, and the results were disastrous for the area.

Effect on Mexico's Criminal Environment

Beyond their direct conflict, the competition between the CJNG and the Sinaloa Cartel has far-reaching effects. Other cartels were compelled to adjust to the shifting dynamics as they struggled for power, which caused changes in alliances, tactics, and territory. The allocation of power among numerous criminal organisations was altered by this cascading effect.

Government Action and Repression

The Mexican government took more decisive action against both cartels as a result of the growing competition. Law enforcement initiatives concentrated on destroying their organisational structures, upsetting their workflow, and focusing on their money networks. However, these efforts were hampered by the cartels' elusiveness and adaptability.

Changing Alliances and Strategies

As the conflict raged on, both cartels changed their tactics. The Sinaloa Cartel, on the other hand, aimed to reclaim its former dominance as the CJNG maintained its efforts to grow abroad. In an effort to anticipate and thwart cartel movements, law enforcement authorities were kept on their toes by the constantly shifting terrain of alliances and power relationships.

The conflict between the CJNG and the Sinaloa Cartel is evidence of how dynamic and intricate Mexico's drug cartel system is. It illuminates the strategic acumen, tenacity, and resolve of various criminal organisations as they compete for dominance, permanently changing the power dynamics in Mexico's criminal underworld.

CHAPTER 7

Government Repression and Increasing Violence

The ongoing history of Mexico's drug cartels shows that the government's attempts to combat organised crime have been both successful and difficult. This chapter explores the many tactics the Mexican government has used to fight the drug cartels as well as the rising bloodshed that has characterised this protracted conflict.

Initiatives for militarization and law enforcement

The Mexican government launched a number of militarised measures to drug cartels' hegemonic influence in order to weaken it. In order to decapitate cartel leadership, seize assets, and stymie operations, joint military and police operations were initiated in a number of locations.

These measures heralded a shift in the fight against organised crime towards more forceful methods.

Successes and Failures

Mixed results came from the government's efforts to combat drug cartels. Although certain notable arrests and convictions were hailed as successes, the entrenched nature of cartel control frequently resulted in failures. Cartels used their abundant resources to maintain control over territory and avoid capture while adapting to law enforcement tactics.

Increasing Violence

As drug cartels responded against government interference and rival factions, violence spiked at the same time as crackdowns on the organisations. Communities were caught in the crossfire as a result of the tit-for-tat battles, which intensified the fatalities. The violence not only presented a major obstacle for law enforcement, but it also had severe social and economic effects.

Concerns for Human Rights

Concerns about violations of human rights and fatalities among civilians increased as the government intensified its campaign against drug gangs. Concerns regarding the tactics used by security forces were raised in the wake of reports of extrajudicial murders, missing persons cases, and disproportionate use of force. The Mexican government now faces a difficult problem in trying to strike a balance between the need for security and upholding fundamental rights.

Effects on Communities

Communities all around Mexico were devastated by the escalating violence and government crackdowns. During cartel conflicts and government enforcement operations, innocent bystanders frequently found themselves in the crosshairs. In many of the conflict-affected areas, displacement, fear, and trauma became prevalent.

Adapting Strategies

The Mexican government changed its tactics throughout time in response to the complexity of the drug cartel issue. The focus of efforts shifted to solving underlying socioeconomic issues that aided cartel influence and recruitment. This more comprehensive strategy aims to give disadvantaged groups alternative alternatives and lessen the appeal of criminal behaviour.

The complexity of this multifaceted conflict is shown by the government's ongoing fight against drug cartels. Although the conflict's trajectory has been determined by victories and setbacks, the effects on communities and the welfare of the country continue to take centre stage. We learn more about the intricate interaction of power, brutality, and the pursuit of justice in Mexico's struggle against organised crime as we move through this historical period.

CHAPTER 8

International Links and Drug Trade Routes

The global scope of drug cartel operations and the complicated trade routes they build are crucial factors in the interconnected universe of these organisations. This chapter explores the extensive network of drug trade channels that crosses continents and the global links that the Mexican drug cartels maintain.

Mexican Cartels' Global Reach

Mexican drug cartels have links that extend well beyond Mexico's borders, transcending national boundaries. These organisations have forged alliances with criminal organisations operating in a number of nations, giving them access to new markets, the ability to obtain precursor chemicals, and the ability to build distribution systems.

Joint Ventures and Alliances

Criminal groups in other nations, including those in the United States, Colombia, and Central American countries, have forged partnerships with cartels like the CJNG and the Sinaloa Cartel. Through these partnerships, the cartels are able to take advantage of the knowledge and assets of their allies, which facilitates the trafficking of drugs and other illegal commodities.

Transportation Routes

Mexico serves as a key transshipment hub for drug trafficking due to its advantageous geographic position. This advantage has been seized by cartels, who now transport illegal narcotics using a large network of land, sea, and air routes. Drugs coming from South America frequently pass via Central America on their way to Mexico, where they are then shipped to the United States and other countries.

Infiltration and Corruption

Corruption and infiltration frequently help Mexican cartels expand their worldwide influence. Cartels have found ways to get beyond identification and enforcement procedures, including buying the loyalty of government employees and paying law enforcement officers. Their control over the routes used for the drug trade is further cemented by this unscrupulous network.

Financial Networks and Money Laundering

Drug trafficking revenues are frequently hidden through the world's intricate financial systems. Cartels invest in legitimate companies, properties, and other assets, making it difficult to track down and collect their illegally acquired wealth. The durability and resiliency of the cartels' operations are aided by these financial networks.

Global Effect

The effects of the Mexican drug cartels' global ties are extensive. Drug abuse, addiction, and violence are all consequences of the flow of narcotics into international markets. Additionally, the enormous revenues made from these operations are used to finance additional criminal activity, which exacerbates social and security issues in numerous nations.

We learn more about the cartels' propensity for adapting, cooperating, and finding weaknesses on a global scale as we delve deeper into the complex web of international relationships and drug transport channels. In order to effectively combat the multifarious threat posed by Mexican drug cartels, international cooperation is necessary, as this chapter emphasises.

CHAPTER 9

Socioeconomic Effects of Cartel Activity

Beyond the headlines of conflict and bloodshed, the actions of the Mexican drug gangs have had significant macroeconomic repercussions. This chapter explores the extensive effects that cartel activity has on Mexican neighbourhoods, economy, and the social fabric.

Undermining institutions and governance

Influence from cartels frequently undermines the basis of law and order. Corrupt authorities who are under the sway of the cartels fail to uphold the law, provide basic services, or maintain security. Communities become more susceptible to cartel control as a result of this loss in institutional trust, which also leads to a feeling of lawlessness.

Economic Dependency and Disruption

Local economies are harmed by cartel activity in many different ways. Businesses are scared away by extortion and violence, which hinders economic progress. Some communities grow reliant on cartel activity, turning to the drug trade for work and revenue when there aren't many legitimate possibilities.

Forced and Displaced Migration

As cartel violence worsens, a large number of people and families are compelled to leave their homes and either become internally displaced or seek safety overseas. This uprooting fuels an unstable cycle and exacerbates the problems faced by communities caught in the crossfire of cartel wars.

Community cohesion and the social fabric

The social fabric of communities can deteriorate when cartels are present. Social ties can be damaged and established norms might be upset by fear, mistrust, and the normalisation of violence. On mental health, family structures, and social dynamics, this has a lasting effect.

Effects on recruitment and youth

Youth who are weak are frequently taken advantage of by cartels, who provide them a feeling of direction, community, and stability. Young people can become dangerously attracted to the promise of rapid money and status, which feeds the cycle of violence and cartel recruitment.

Mitigation Strategies

The socioeconomic effects of cartel activity must be addressed through a multifaceted strategy. In order to restore trust and resilience, this entails addressing poverty and a lack of opportunities, making investments in education and career training, and encouraging community involvement.

Concerns for Human Rights

The socioeconomic difficulties that affected communities experience are made worse by the human rights abuses that frequently go hand in hand with cartel activities, including as forced recruitment, kidnappings, and extortion. Protection of human rights must be given top priority in a complete response, together with consideration of the wider implications.

Our examination of the complex effects of cartel activity on Mexico's society and economy makes it evident that more than just law enforcement is needed to combat the issue. Building a safer, more prosperous future for Mexico requires a comprehensive strategy that tackles the underlying causes of cartel dominance and helps impacted communities.

CHAPTER 10

Efforts and Plans to Stop Drug Cartel Invasion

Law enforcement agencies, governmental entities, and civil society have continuously tried to thwart the incursions and influence of these criminal organisations. This chapter explores the different initiatives and plans put in place to fight the cartels and safeguard Mexico's communities.

Consolidating Law Enforcement

To better combat cartels, law enforcement organisations have undergone substantial modifications. The goal of specialised units, intelligence-sharing methods, and training programmes is to provide cops with the knowledge and tools necessary to effectively combat organised crime.

Takedowns of targeted operations and leadership

One important tactic has been targeted operations aimed at arresting or removing cartel leaders. High-profile arrests and convictions destabilise the leadership and operational structures of the cartels. However, due to these organisations' adaptability, it frequently takes time and effort to reduce their influence.

Engagement and Empowerment of the Community

It is essential to empower local communities to fend off cartel control. Programmes that foster social cohesion, citizen patrols, and community policing initiatives all contribute to preventing cartel infiltration into neighbourhoods. Communities with more power are better able to report suspicious activity and reject illegal activity.

Anti-Corruption Initiatives

It is crucial to address corruption in government and law enforcement organisations. Rebuilding confidence between communities and those in charge of upholding law and order is made possible by anti-corruption task forces, transparency campaigns, and systems to hold authorities accountable.

Vulnerable Populations Alternatives

A proactive method of preventing cartel recruitment is to offer vulnerable populations—especially young people—alternative possibilities. Programmes for education, career development, and job creation divert people away from criminal activity and provide a route to successful employment.

Cooperation between nations

International cooperation is crucial since cartels are transnational in nature. The coordinated response to organised crime is strengthened via intelligence sharing, cooperative operations, and extraditions. Cooperative actions destroy financial networks and undermine drug trade routes.

Security and human rights must be balanced.

It is crucial to strike a careful balance between protecting security and upholding human rights. Protection of citizens and obedience to the law must come first in efforts to fight cartels. Finding this balance makes guarantee that the war against cartels is fair and successful.

We learn about the intricacy of this ongoing conflict as we examine the various tactics used to thwart drug cartel incursions. The combined efforts of numerous stakeholders are crucial in altering Mexico's trajectory and building a safer, more resilient country, from law enforcement activities to community empowerment.

CONCLUSION

The Takeaways and the Future Directions

A tapestry of intricate narratives develops as we draw to a close our examination of the largest incursions by Mexico's drug gangs. The tales of political squabbles, bloodshed, and societal effects have created a tapestry that shows both the tenacity of the Mexican people and the difficulties posed by organised crime.

We have seen the bold power moves of cartels like the Zetas, the strategic supremacy of the Sinaloa Cartel, the perverse ideology of the Knights Templar, and the quick rise of the CJNG throughout these pages. These cartels, each with their own unique traits, have influenced Mexico's history by leaving their imprints on its societies, economies, and systems of government.

The fragile balance between governmental authority and cartel opposition was demonstrated in the Battle of Culiacan. As authorities struggle with the complex dynamics of cartel influence, we have witnessed the evolution of government measures, from military to community participation. The need for international cooperation has been highlighted by efforts to confront the cartels' global reach and the effects they have on communities.

We have seen glimpses of Mexico's towns' strength, people's resiliency, and the resolve of those fighting the cartels' power amid the stories of violence and destruction. Communities have united, and programmes promoting empowerment, education, and other employment options have showed promise in ending the cycle of cartel recruitment.

We are reminded as we draw to a conclusion of the continuous nature of the war against drug cartels. The historical lessons highlight the value of an all-encompassing strategy that covers not only law enforcement but also the socioeconomic elements that impact cartel influence. It is still difficult to strike a balance between security and human rights, but doing so is essential to creating a just and stable Mexico.

Continued collaboration between law enforcement, governmental entities, civil society, and international partners is necessary for the future. A better future is possible if everyone works together to destroy financial networks, obstruct drug trade routes, and give vulnerable communities sustainable alternatives.

In the end, the story of Mexico's drug cartels is a monument to the fortitude of a nation and its people rather than just an account of invasion and bloodshed. Mexico can create the conditions for a safer and more successful future by acknowledging the past, taking lessons from it, and resolving to live in the present without the influence of organised crime.

Authors' note

I'm humbled by the opportunity to share these tales with you as I come to a conclusion on this journey through the history of Mexico's drug cartels. My intention in authoring this book was to shed light on the intricate and varied nature of the problems that the Mexican drug cartels bring.

I've been impressed by the Mexican people's tenacity and persistent resolve to vanquish the shadow of organised crime throughout the process. The resilience and strength of the human spirit are demonstrated by the tales of towns banding together, police departments changing their tactics, and people working towards a better future.

I hope you've also noticed the glimmer of optimism and the possibility for change despite how dismal the stories of bloodshed and power conflicts are. I really believe that by grasping the complexities of the past, we may pave the way for a more secure and safe future for Mexico.

I want to convey my appreciation to those who contributed their thoughts, the historians who meticulously recorded these incidents, and the numerous people battling the grip of drug cartels. The groundwork for this book was laid by their experiences and initiatives.

I endulge you to consider the lessons drawn from Mexico's past as we turn the final page and to picture a world without cartels determining the country's future. May this investigation spur debate, movement, and a shared dedication to creating a better future for Mexico and its people.

I appreciate you coming along on the ride.

NOTES

NOTES